THE LOLLY BOOK

50
FRUITY, FROSTY, NATURAL
FLAVOURS FOR ALL AGES

KARIS & DOMINIC GESUA

PHOTOGRAPHY BY RITA PLATTS

KYLE BOOKS

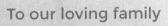
To our loving family

CONTENTS

INTRODUCTION

Welcome to *The Lolly Book*!

We created this book because we wanted to share our recipes with everyone and to show that ice lollies can be a great healthy snack, a fun treat or an easy and super quick-to-prepare dessert option.

When we started on our lolly adventure, we just made lollies for our friends and family. LICKALIX was born because we wanted to follow our dream and set up a company that we could be proud of, one based on principles and an ethos in which we truly believed. We tried to buy lollies like the ones we were making at home for when we were out and about or just didn't have time to make them ourselves, but we couldn't find any. We wanted other people to have the choice of a healthy frozen treat and so LICKALIX came to fruition, where we hand-make natural ice lollies using real whole fruit for all the family to enjoy.

As we researched lollies, we learned that they are believed to have originated in Mexico. According to legend, Aztec emperors used to take the snow from the mountains and combine it with a delicious mix of fresh fruit. In the early twentieth century, ice lollies spread across North America, with lots of artisan producers popping up and making creative frozen treats. In the last few years, a wonderful trend of using fresh fruit ingredients and unusual flavours has spread across the globe to open peoples' eyes to how delicious ice lollies can be.

Ice lollies are called different things all across the globe. Mexicans and Spanish speakers call them *paletas*, Australians call them ice blocks, Americans call them pops or ice pops and recently we learnt that a lot of people from Liverpool in the UK call them lolly ices! It doesn't matter what you call them, get some great ingredients, blend them up, freeze 'em and enjoy them!

We actually started our lolly journey many years ago – ice lollies are nostalgic; we remember making them with our mums each summer. We would get the plastic moulds out of the drawer where they had been living since the last summer and fill them with apple or orange juice, feeling very proud eating the lollies that we had made ourselves.

For us, lollies are all about using real whole fruits and quality ingredients. They're about getting creative and thinking outside the lolly mould – about textures, how they look, different tastes on the palate and how to present them when serving. We also experiment with adding alcohol to make a grown-ups-only treat – we call them poptails...

So turn the page, get creative and start your own lolly adventure!

Lots of lolly love,

Karis & Domini

LOLLY-MAKING TIPS

The ingredients

For us, it's about getting all the goodness out of the fruit. If you don't like the seeds or skin from berries, then you can push the mixture through a fine sieve, but by doing this you will lose some nutrients and fibre, which are good for you. When using juice, try to squeeze it yourself and use as much of the pulp as possible. If you need to buy it, try to get the kind that still has the pulp in it and says 'not from concentrate'.

The quality of ingredients is very important and makes a real difference to the finished product, as it isn't cooked. By not cooking the ingredients, the nutrients stay in the lollies, which is a healthier way to eat. It also simplifies things and saves you time! We prefer to source fruit and veg from our local farmers' market, so we know where it comes from, and help local businesses. We also buy organic and Fairtrade whenever we can.

What you'll need to make the ice lollies

- Lolly moulds
- Lolly sticks, if you want them to feel like the ones you ate as a child!
- Lolly stick-holder (see opposite)
- Blender
- Container with a spout
- Chopping board, knives and peeler
- Spoons and weighing scales
- Greaseproof paper
- Air-tight plastic containers
- Deep container or sink (to de-mould)
- And a freezer!

Blending

A lot of ingredients are whizzed together. Simply use your regular kitchen blender, a hand-held blender or a NutriBullet.

Sugar

Lots of recipes call for melting the sugar first, but we are all about simplicity and not creating extra steps if you don't need them. Instead, you can just blend up the sugar with the other ingredients. Ensure it has been blended fully by tasting the mixture with a teaspoon; you will be able to feel a grainy texture if the sugar hasn't all dissolved. If necessary, simply re-blend until the sugar is all mixed in.

Lots of people ask why we add sugar. Basically, when foods are frozen, their flavour profile changes; adding a little bit of sugar enhances the flavour and helps to give a nice texture. Take our recipes as a guide and you can add less or more sugar depending on how sweet you want your lollies. Always taste the mixture before freezing and you will start to tell how sweet you like it compared with the frozen lolly. In the Healthy Kicks section there are recipes that don't require any sugar. For more information on sugar see page 11.

Pouring into moulds

It's best to pour from a container with a spout. This enables you to pour more accurately, which is important when doing layers. You will need to leave a gap of about 1–1.5cm at the top of the mould, otherwise the mixture will expand out of the top and be hard to de-mould. Wipe off any lolly mixture coming out of the mould.

Sticks

Almost all moulds come with plastic tops with the stick built in. We like to use wooden sticks as we think they look better and make the lollies feel more nostalgic. You can easily buy sticks online. If you do use them, have fun: write little messages or jokes on the part of the stick that you hold, write guests' names on them, decorate with ribbons or other lovely items to add the wow factor when you serve them. If using wooden sticks, you will need to make your own stick-holder. Either cover the moulds with foil or clingfilm, which will keep the sticks in place when freezing, or cut a cover out of cardboard, which we prefer. To do this, take a piece of cardboard – for example a cereal packet – and cut a cover to the same shape as the opening of your moulds. Mark the centre of each opening on the cover with a pencil line. Then, using a pair of scissors or craft knife, cut through the line to make a small hole. You can then put your wooden sticks through the slits and they will be held in place.

Dipping and toppings

Have fun and dip your lollies in chocolate and toppings. Some recipes already have these, but experiment and try out dips and sprinkles on any of your lollies. Buy quality chocolate and break it up into a microwavable container. The easiest way to melt the chocolate is to microwave it in 10–30 second bursts and stir after each time; the chocolate can easily burn so keep an eye on it. Or you can melt it in a heatproof bowl over a saucepan of barely simmering water. If using milk or dark chocolate, add 1 teaspoon of coconut oil per 100g of chocolate when melting, to make it set better. Or drizzle the chocolate over your lollies; you can even write or draw a picture! For toppings, get creative and try out whatever comes to mind. Crush up your chosen topping into a container and dip the lollies straight away once they have been dipped into the chocolate. Try out different nuts, chopped fruit, crushed cereal bits and cake toppings such as hundreds and thousands or edible glitter.

Different lolly looks

Some recipes take you through different looks, such as multi-coloured layers that require freezing in between pouring the layers. You could create angled layers by tipping the moulds to one side in the freezer; prop them at an angle with a bag of peas. Creating layers does take a little more time, so there are some recipes with 'quick layers', freezing the lolly in one go. These layers won't look perfect, but they are quick to make. There are also recipes with swirls, which don't take that much more time to make, but look amazing.

Using alcohol

Make some truly adult fun treats and desserts and add some alcohol to your lollies to turn them into poptails! You need to be careful how much you add because alcohol doesn't actually freeze. Instead, the poptails will have a nice texture and will be slightly softer to eat.

Freezing

It's best to place the moulds in the back of your freezer, where it is coldest. This will freeze the lollies more quickly and produce a better texture. It's best to do this overnight, but depending on your freezer, the lollies may be ready within 4–6 hours. The freezing time depends on a number of factors, so always check all the lollies are completely frozen before de-moulding.

De-moulding

We find the best way to de-mould the lollies is to fill up a container or kitchen sink with warm (not hot) water to the height of your moulds. Take your lollies and swish them back and forth in the water for 3–10 seconds, taking care not to spill any water into the moulds. The swishing motion allows the water to flow all around the moulds if they come together as a set. Alternatively, you can run them under warm water. Try to remove them from the mould by pulling gently upwards in a straight line; if they don't come out at once, place them back in the warm water bath for a few more seconds and try again. If you pull too hard and the outside is not slightly melted all over, the lolly can break and part of it will stay in the mould. Creamier lollies tend to be harder to de-mould, so be patient.

Storage

If you don't eat your ice lollies straight after de-moulding, put them back in the freezer straight away. Putting them in the freezer for just 30 minutes will make the lollies hold their shape better and melt more slowly than if you ate them straight after de-moulding.

The best way to store the de-moulded ice lollies is in a plastic container with a good airtight lid. Place greaseproof paper between layers of ice lollies to prevent them from sticking to each other. You will find that ice crystals will form if your freezer isn't that great. This is fine – it is just some of the water molecules moving from inside to outside the lollies as the temperature of your freezer fluctuates. Just dust off the icy snow or run under cold water before serving. If you don't store the lollies properly protected in a container, they can get freezer burn, dehydrate and not taste as good. If well wrapped, the lollies will keep in your freezer for weeks.

Milk alternatives

At LICKALIX we feel it's important to make sure everyone can enjoy our lollies, so we use coconut milk instead of cow's milk. You can use a range of alternatives or just stick to cow's milk. When you see that a recipe calls for milk or yogurt, feel free to experiment and use your preferred milky base. Coconut milk works well as it is really creamy and the fat is good fat. Milk is also good because of the calcium you get, but if you need a dairy-free alternative you can also try almond milk, which naturally tastes slightly sweet and is good for you. We find coconut and almond milk work the best, but you could also try rice milk, oat milk, hemp milk or soya milk. You can actually make your own almond or rice milk, if you like.

When it comes to using yogurt, try to keep the same consistency. For a dairy-free alternative, try using coconut cream or coconut yogurt. Always try to get the sugar-free option and use the one that works best for you and your family.

Sugar alternatives

We explained on page 8 why lollies need added sugar. We don't believe in cutting it out of your diet completely, but we do believe in eating everything in moderation. When it comes to sugar, we prefer to use unrefined organic and Fairtrade cane because the refining process strips out some of the nutrients.

There are alternatives, though almost all natural sugar alternatives still contain sucrose, the same as sugar. Popular ones are agave nectar, honey, coconut palm sugar or palmyra jiggery. Each has its own benefits and negatives, but all contain sucrose, and so they still need to be used in moderation – do your research before using them. Another alternative is to use grape juice; however, this has been processed, which removes some of the nutrients such as the fibre that you would get if you ate the whole fruit. In juice form it also has a higher concentration of sugar than the whole fruit.

But don't worry – our recipes have a low amount of added sugar and make a healthy and natural alternative snack or dessert for the whole family to enjoy.

EVERYDAY LOLLIES

BERRY LEMONADE

Little frozen blueberry bites in a tangy, fresh strawberry lolly.

SERVES   PREP   FREEZING

4   **5**   **6**
MINS   HRS

OR OVERNIGHT

160g strawberries, hulled and chopped

40ml freshly squeezed lemon juice

40g natural unrefined cane sugar

a small handful of blueberries (the smaller berries work best)

Put the strawberries, lemon juice, 60ml of water and sugar in a blender and whizz together.

Divide half the mixture between the moulds, then place a few blueberries in each one.

Top up the moulds with the remaining mixture, leaving a 1.5cm gap at the top.

Place a few more blueberries in the mould (you can use a stick to scatter the blueberries, if you like).

Insert the sticks with the stick-holders and place in the freezer.

FUN FACT

A strawberry isn't actually a berry, but a banana is!

EVERYDAY LOLLIES
14

PEACH & BLACKBERRY

A refreshing summer lolly; sweet peaches and tangy blackberries suspended in the lolly make it irresistible.

SERVES **4** PREP **5** MINS FREEZING **6** HRS

OR OVERNIGHT

200g ripe peaches, unpeeled, stoned and cut into chunks

4 teaspoons natural unrefined cane sugar

4–8 blackberries, sliced into 5mm thick circles

Put the peaches, sugar and 80ml of water in a blender and whizz together.

Divide the mixture between the moulds, leaving a 1.5cm gap at the top.

Place the blackberry slices in the moulds, (use a spare stick to move the blackberries into a nice pattern, if you like). Try to place the blackberry slices near to the sides of the moulds – this way, when you de-mould the lollies, the blackberries will be visible.

Insert the sticks with the stick-holders and place in the freezer.

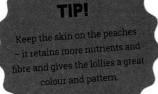

TIP!

Keep the skin on the peaches – it retains more nutrients and fibre and gives the lollies a great colour and pattern.

PINEAPPLE LIME ZINGER

This super-quick-to-prepare and easy-to-make lolly is perfect whenever you're in need of something refreshing and tangy.

SERVES 4

PREP 5 MINS

FREEZING 6 HRS

OR OVERNIGHT

160g pineapple, peeled and cut into small pieces (about ⅓ of a pineapple)

20ml freshly squeezed lime juice

4 teaspoons natural unrefined cane sugar

Put the pineapple, lime juice, sugar and 100ml of water in a blender and whizz together.

Divide the mixture between the moulds, leaving a 1cm gap at the top.

Insert the sticks with the stick-holders and place in the freezer.

TIP!

Want to treat your taste buds to something a little different? Increase the amount of pineapple to 200g and add 8 medium basil leaves. We know it sounds a little crazy but try it... it works!

DOUBLE TROUBLE STRAWBERRY

A two-tone, two-taste lolly that the whole family will enjoy.

SERVES   PREP   FREEZING

4   **10** MINS   **3** HRS

+ OVERNIGHT OR
AT LEAST 6 HOURS

180g strawberries, hulled and chopped

70ml milk, coconut milk or almond milk

4 teaspoons natural unrefined cane sugar

a few extra strawberry slices and small pieces (optional)

Put 100g of the chopped strawberries, the milk and 2 teaspoons of the sugar in a blender and whizz together.

Half-fill the moulds (with this light-pink mixture). At this point, you can make the lollies look even better by adding a couple of strawberry slices to each mould, as close to the sides of the mould as possible.

Put the lollies in the freezer for about 3 hours, or until the mixture is slightly hard, then take them out for the second part.

Put the remaining chopped strawberries and sugar with 50ml of water in a blender and whizz together. If you want to give added texture to the lollies, put in the small strawberry pieces and stir.

Pour this second strawberry mixture into the moulds, leaving a 1cm gap to the top. Insert the sticks with the stick-holders and place in the freezer.

TIP!

No time to freeze layers? Pour the second layer carefully, not from a height, to make a swirl.

Look out for perfectly shaped strawberries that look like hearts when sliced!

MANGO LASSI

A perfect lolly any time of the day, but try having this as a dessert after a spicy meal to refresh and cool down your taste buds. To make them look extra special, try doing some quick layers...

SERVES **4**

PREP **5-15** MINS

FREEZING **6** HRS

OR OVERNIGHT

80g mango, peeled and chopped

4 teaspoons natural unrefined cane sugar

140g natural yogurt

TIP!

Did you know that mangoes come from the same plant family as cashews and pistachios?

You can make this lolly recipe in two ways:

Option 1: If you're pushed for time...
Whizz all the ingredients together with 60ml of water in a blender, then divide the mixture between the moulds, leaving a 1cm gap at the top. Insert the sticks with the stick-holders and place in the freezer.

Option 2: If you have a little more time...
Whizz the mango, 2 teaspoons of the sugar and 60ml of water in a blender and set aside. Then whizz the yogurt and the remaining sugar in a blender and set aside in a bowl.

Pour the mango mixture into each mould until it is a quarter full. Next, carefully spoon in a layer of the yogurt mixture; you want it to sit on top of the mango layer, so don't pour it.

Alternate the mango and yogurt mixtures until you have four layers, leaving a 1cm gap at the top. Insert the sticks with the stick-holders and place in the freezer.

BLUEBERRY & BERGAMOT

You might not have thought about these two flavours together...
but it works so well. Give it a try.

SERVES 4

PREP 5 MINS.

FREEZING 6 HRS
OR OVERNIGHT

1 earl grey tea bag

200ml boiling water

100g blueberries

5 teaspoons natural unrefined cane sugar

Soak the earl grey tea bag in the boiling water for approximately 10–30 seconds, or until the water has turned a deepish brown colour.

Put the tea, blueberries and sugar in a blender and whizz together.

Divide the mixture between the moulds, leaving a 1cm gap at the top.

Insert the sticks with the stick-holders and place in the freezer.

TRY THIS

Planning on serving afternoon tea? Mix it up and serve these lollies after the cakes!

TANGY PAPAYA

Try this tropical tangy ice lolly! A small papaya contains about 300% of your recommended daily vitamin C and aids digestion, so one of these is perfect to boost your intake or as a light dessert after a big meal.

SERVES **PREP** **FREEZING**

 4 **5** MINS **6** HRS

OR OVERNIGHT

200g papaya, peeled, deseeded and chopped

20ml freshly squeezed lemon juice

4 teaspoons natural unrefined cane sugar

Put all the ingredients and 60ml of water in a blender and whizz together.

Divide the mixture between the moulds, leaving a 1cm gap at the top.

Insert the sticks with the stick-holders and place in the freezer.

TROPICAL SURPRISE

A refreshing lolly with suspended sweet mango bites. Totally tropical and healthy. Watermelons are a good source of fibre, potassium, and vitamins A and C.

SERVES **PREP** **FREEZING**

 4 **10** MINS **6** HRS

OR OVERNIGHT

200g watermelon, rind and seeds removed

0-3 teaspoons natural unrefined cane sugar

a handful of small diced mango pieces

Whizz the watermelon in a blender. Taste the mixture to see if you need to add any extra sugar, then add a little at a time; the amount will depend on the fruit.

Divide half the mixture between the moulds, then place a few mango pieces in each mould. Top up with the remaining watermelon mixture, leaving a 1.5cm gap.

Add a few more mango pieces to the moulds (use a stick to spread the pieces, if you like). Insert the sticks with the stick-holders and place in the freezer.

STRAWBERRY & COCONUT SWIRL

Give this recipe a go if you want to make lollies with swirls.
Such good-looking lollies!

SERVES 4

PREP 7 MINS

FREEZING 6 HRS

OR OVERNIGHT

100g strawberries, hulled and chopped

5 teaspoons natural unrefined cane sugar

100ml coconut milk

TIP!
Try a cherry version; just
replace the strawberries with
100g of cherries,
stones removed.

Put the strawberries, 2 teaspoons of the sugar and 50ml of water in a blender and whizz together, then set aside. Whizz together the coconut milk, 20ml of water and the remaining sugar, and set aside.

Pour the strawberry mixture into the moulds until they are about half full. Carefully pour in the coconut mixture next, swirling it on top of the strawberry layer and leaving a 1cm gap at the top. Pour gently so the coconut hits the sides of the moulds first, or you will end up with a one-colour lolly.

Before inserting the sticks, check the swirls and, if you like, gently place a spare stick in each mould and slowly move it up and down and then from side to side to mix the swirls further. Insert the sticks with the stick-holders and place in the freezer.

PARTY
TIME

WATERMELON & KIWI

This lolly looks like a frozen slice of watermelon!

SERVES **4**

PREP **15** MINS

FREEZING **3** HRS

+ OVERNIGHT OR
AT LEAST 6 HOURS

170g watermelon, rind and seeds removed, chopped (dark green ones with faint stripes often have fewer seeds)

0–4 teaspoons natural unrefined cane sugar

50g kiwi, peeled

Put the watermelon in a blender and whizz. Taste the mixture to see if you need to add any extra sugar; this will depend on the sweetness of the fruit. Add a little sugar at a time until the sweetness is to your taste.

Divide the watermelon mixture between the moulds until they are three-quarters full.

Insert the sticks with the stick-holders and place in the freezer.

Freeze for about 3 hours or until the top of the mixture is quite frozen.

For the second layer, whizz the kiwi and 25ml of water in a blender, again adding sugar to taste. How much sugar you need depends on how ripe the kiwis are; the riper they are the less sugar you'll need.

Take off the stick-holders and pour the kiwi mixture into the moulds, leaving a 1cm gap at the top. There is no need to put the stick-holder back on. Return the moulds to the freezer.

TIP!
Buy your kiwis at least 4 days in advance because they ripen slowly

SHANDY ON A STICK

A great refreshing addition to a barbecue or garden party.

SERVES **PREP** **FREEZING**

 4 **5** MINS **6** HRS

OR OVERNIGHT

80ml beer

25ml freshly squeezed lemon juice

40g natural unrefined cane sugar

Put all the ingredients and 155ml of water in a blender and whizz together.

Depending on the beer, you may need to let the mixture settle so the bubbles from the beer go down.

Divide the mixture between the moulds, leaving a 1cm gap at the top.

Insert the sticks with the stick-holders and place in the freezer.

TIP!

Try this recipe using different beers and see which is your favourite. Ours is a light beer that has hints of bergamot in it... delicious!

STRAWBERRY CHEESECAKE

Try this lolly twist on a classic for an easy dessert to make for a dinner party. It will leave a smile on everyone's faces.

SERVES	PREP	FREEZING
4	10 MINS	6 HRS

OR OVERNIGHT

90g strawberries, hulled and chopped

150g light cream cheese

12 teaspoons natural unrefined cane sugar

a few extra small strawberry pieces (optional)

2 plain biscuits, crumbled (Hobnobs work best with their oaty crunch)

Put the strawberries, 90g of the cream cheese and 8 teaspoons of the sugar with 40ml of water in a blender and whizz together. For extra texture, if desired add the strawberry pieces to the mixture and stir.

Divide the mixture between the moulds until three-quarters full. In a separate bowl, stir the remaining cream cheese and sugar with 20ml of water and three-quarters of the crumbled biscuits.

Spoon the creamy crumble mix into each mould, leaving a 1cm gap at the top, then sprinkle the remaining biscuit crumbs on the top of each lolly and lightly press down so they don't fall out when you de-mould the lollies.

Insert the sticks with the stick-holders and place in the freezer.

TIP!

Want to make the lolly a little lighter? Replace the cream cheese and water with 210ml of yogurt, milk or almond milk and half the amount of sugar.

PARTY TIME

BLACKBERRY HOPSICLE

The blackberries give a great intense colour and the
beer makes this lolly surprisingly creamy. Give it a try.

SERVES | PREP | FREEZING

4 | **5** MINS | **6** HRS

OR OVERNIGHT

80ml pale ale

190g blackberries

10ml freshly squeezed lemon juice

8 teaspoons natural unrefined cane sugar

Put all the ingredients in a blender and whizz
together.

Depending on the beer, you may need to let
the mixture settle and the bubbles go down.

Divide the mixture between the moulds,
leaving a 1cm gap at the top.

Insert the sticks with the stick-holders and
place in the freezer.

FUN FACT

Blackberries
have one of the
highest antioxidant
levels of all fruits.

WHITE WINE SANGRIA

Serve this lolly to wow your friends and garnish with any leftover edible flowers!

SERVES	PREP	FREEZING
4	10 MINS	6 HRS

OR OVERNIGHT

80ml white wine (the sweeter the better)

220ml white grape juice

a small handful of hulled and diced strawberries

a small handful of pitted and diced peach

a small handful of diced blueberries

a small handful of peeled, diced orange

a small handful of diced red grapes

a small handful of chopped fresh mint

a few edible flowers (optional)

In a jug, stir together the wine and grape juice. Place a few pieces each of the fruit and mint into each mould. Pour the wine mixture into the moulds, leaving a 3cm gap at the top.

Place more of the fruit, mint and flowers, if using, into each mould. If needed, top up the moulds with any remaining wine mixture to leave just a 1cm gap at the top.

Insert the sticks with the stick-holders and place in the freezer.

Try tying ribbons around each lolly stick before presenting them to your guests to make the lollies look extra special!

ITALIAN STRAWBERRY

When we first put this on the menu our customers said,
'If ever a lolly tasted like a pizza... this is it!'

SERVES 4 **PREP** 7 MINS **FREEZING** 6 HRS

OR OVERNIGHT

180g strawberries, chopped

6 medium basil leaves

35g natural unrefined cane sugar

a drizzle of balsamic glaze syrup

Put the strawberries, basil leaves and sugar with 80ml of water in a blender and whizz together.

Divide the mixture between the moulds, leaving a 1cm gap at the top.

Drizzle a little bit of the balsamic glaze into each mould.

Insert the sticks with the stick-holders and place in the freezer.

TIP!
If you can't get hold of balsamic glaze, then you can add about 10 drops of balsamic vinegar to the ingredients as you whizz them together in the blender.

MANGO & POMEGRANATE

This great-looking lolly is the perfect light dessert to serve – your friends and family won't have seen anything like it!

SERVES 4
PREP 10 MINS
FREEZING 6 HRS
OR OVERNIGHT

200g mango, peeled and chopped

4 teaspoons natural unrefined sugar

4–8 teaspoons pomegranate seeds

Put the mango, sugar and 100ml of water in a blender and whizz together.

Divide the mixture between the moulds, leaving a 2cm gap at the top.

Spoon 1–2 teaspoons of pomegranate seeds into each mould.

If needed, top up the moulds with any remaining mango mix to leave a 1cm gap at the top.

Insert the sticks with the stick-holders and place in the freezer.

FUN FACT

Pomegranates contain around three times more antioxidants than green tea!

CUCUMBER, LIME & DILL PALATE CLEANSER

If you are planning a meal and need a palate cleanser between courses, this is a fun way to refresh everyone's mouths.

SERVES **4**

PREP **5** MINS

FREEZING **6** HRS

OR OVERNIGHT

300g cucumber, peeled and chopped

40ml freshly squeezed lime juice

4 pinches (about ¼ teaspoon) of dried or 2 pinches of fresh dill

Put all the ingredients in a blender and whizz together. Divide the mixture between the moulds, leaving a 1cm gap at the top.

Insert the sticks with the stick-holders and place in the freezer.

CARROT POPS

Throwing a garden party where everyone is invited? This recipe doubles up as a refreshing snack for dogs, too!

SERVES **4**

PREP **5** MINS

FREEZING **6** HRS

OR OVERNIGHT

150ml carrot juice

a small handful of peeled and diced cucumber and carrot pieces

In a jug, stir together the carrot juice and 150ml of water. Divide the mixture between the moulds, leaving a 2cm gap at the top.

Place cucumber and carrot pieces into the moulds until there is a 1cm gap at the top. Use a spare stick to evenly spread the pieces around the lollies. Insert the sticks with the stick-holders and place in the freezer.

PARTY TIME

46

FROZEN FRUITY BOWLS

Get everyone involved making their own fruit dessert. Arrange all the ingredients on the table and get creative with sauces and toppings. Go crazy and add whatever you like to the bowl of frozen treats!

SERVES	PREP	FREEZING
10+	20 MINS	0 HRS

FOR THE FRUIT SAUCES

250g strawberries, hulled and chopped

250g mango, peeled and chopped

250g kiwi, peeled and chopped

FOR THE TABLE

ice cubes (1 shop-bought bag or a few frozen trays)

200g strawberries, hulled and cut into small cubes

200g pineapple, peeled and cut into small cubes

5 passion fruit, halved and seeds scooped out

a large handful each of raspberries, blackberries and blueberries

For the fruit sauces, put the strawberries and 100ml of water in a blender and whizz together, then set aside in the fridge. Repeat with the mango and kiwis, blending each fruit separately with 100ml of water.

To set up your frozen fruity bowl table, put the ice cubes into a big serving bowl, put the fruit into small serving bowls and set out jugs of sauces, together with bowls and spoons.

Each time you serve a frozen dessert, whizz the ice to the consistency of a slushy and serve in a bowl.

Then get each person to create their own fruity dessert by topping with the fruit sauce and fruit pieces of choice. Flavours that work well together are kiwi and strawberry; mango, pineapple and passion fruit; and berries. Try combinations of your favourite fruits!

TIP!

This is as much about the presentation and experience as it is the taste. Consider the bowls and jugs you use and how you set out the dessert table. Think about what tablecloth and accessories you can use to dress the table.

PARTY TIME

48

STRAWBERRY, WHITE CHOCOLATE & PISTACHIO

A real crowd-pleaser and looks fantastic!

SERVES 4

PREP 15 MINS

FREEZING 6 HRS

OR OVERNIGHT

200g strawberries, hulled and chopped

4 teaspoons natural unrefined cane sugar

50g white chocolate, broken into pieces

a small bowl of finely chopped pistachios (either blend or use the good old-fashioned trick of placing them between two clean tea towels and use a rolling pin or mallet to crush them!)

TIP!

Choose a container to melt the chocolate in that is tall enough to fit the length of the lolly and just wide enough for the width of the lolly so you use the chocolate most effectively.

Put the strawberries and sugar with 100ml of water in a blender and whizz together. Divide the mixture between the moulds, leaving a 1cm gap at the top. Insert the sticks with the stick-holders and place in the freezer.

When the lollies are fully frozen, put the chocolate into a microwavable container and microwave for 20 seconds and stir; microwave again for 10 seconds and stir. Continue until the chocolate is completely melted, but keep your eye on it as the chocolate can easily burn.

De-mould one lolly at a time and dip it into the melted chocolate at an angle. Allow the excess chocolate to drip off, then dip the lolly into the bowl of chopped pistachios.

Wait until the chocolate has set and serve immediately, or return to the freezer until ready to serve. Repeat with the other lollies.

KIDS'
PARTIES

OCTOPOP

Make these fun lollies that look like octopuses!
The perfect added extra for any underwater-themed party.

SERVES **4** PREP **10** MINS FREEZING **6** HRS

OR OVERNIGHT

300ml white grape juice

a small handful of blueberries

carrot, beetroot or courgette spirals
or thin strands

Divide the grape juice between the moulds, leaving a 2cm gap at the top.

Place a few blueberries into each mould (these are the 'insides' of the octopus). Top up each mould with grape juice leaving a 1cm gap.

Use a spiraliser to create the octopus legs. If you don't have a spiraliser, use a peeler and cut each peel to make thin legs. Place the spirals just inside the moulds and let the rest hang over the outside of the moulds.

Insert the sticks with the stick-holders and place in the freezer. We find the best stick-holder device to use for this lolly is foil, instead of clingfilm or card.

TIP!

Use whatever fruit or veg you like to make the legs of the octopus – the more colourful the better. Consider using citrus peel, apple peel or even strawberry lace sweets!

NUTELLA POPS

A chocolatey favourite with both children and adults.

SERVES 4

PREP 5 MINS

FREEZING 6 HRS OR OVERNIGHT

100g Nutella®

200ml whole milk

4 teaspoons natural unrefined sugar

Put all the ingredients in a blender and whizz together.

Spatula any remaining Nutella that has got stuck to the sides, then divide the mixture between the moulds, leaving a 1cm gap at the top.

Insert the sticks with the stick-holders and place in the freezer.

SWEET SURPRISE

Your favourite sweeties frozen in a dessert!

SERVES 4

PREP 5 MINS

FREEZING 6 HRS OR OVERNIGHT

300ml clear lemonade

a handful of different sweets (we find gummy worms work best)

Divide the lemonade between the moulds, leaving a 3cm gap at the top.

Place some sweets in each mould and top up with lemonade, leaving a 1cm gap at the top.

Insert the sticks with the stick-holders and place in the freezer.

STRAWBERRY MILKSHAKE & COOKIES

Not just for kids' parties, this lolly is for any time and anyone.

SERVES **4**   PREP **7** MINS   FREEZING **6** HRS
OR OVERNIGHT

150g strawberries, hulled and chopped

140ml whole milk

4 teaspoons natural unrefined sugar

4–8 of your favourite cookies

FUN FACT

Did you know that the strawberry is the only fruit to have its seeds on the outside?

Put the strawberries, milk and sugar in a blender and whizz together.

Divide the mixture between the moulds, leaving a 3cm gap at the top.

Either place a whole cookie, if it will fit, into each mould or break up the cookies into pieces and scatter them equally in each mould. You can use a spare stick to arrange the cookie pieces, if you like.

Top up each mould with the milk mixture, leaving a 1cm gap at the top.

Insert the sticks with the stick-holders and place in the freezer.

DIPPING BONANZA

Kids go crazy for this dessert table at a party. They can all have a go at making their own lolly creation... and then have fun eating it, too!

SERVES 16 **PREP** 25 MINS **FREEZING** 6 HRS

OR OVERNIGHT

160g strawberries, hulled and chopped

160g pineapple, peeled and chopped

160g raspberries, chopped

160g cherries, stoned and chopped

16 teaspoons natural unrefined sugar

FOR THE DIPS AND SPRINKLES
100g white chocolate, broken into pieces

100g milk chocolate, broken into pieces

100g dark chocolate, broken into pieces

2 teaspoons coconut oil

various sprinkles and chopped nuts

To make the lollies, whizz each fruit separately with 130ml of water and 4 teaspoons of sugar in a blender. Divide each flavour mixture between four moulds, leaving a 1cm gap at the top. Insert the sticks with the stick-holders and place in the freezer.

When frozen, de-mould and store until ready to use. Prepare the dipping bowls when you are ready to serve the lollies: put each chocolate into a separate microwavable bowl. Add 1 teaspoon of coconut oil to each of the milk and dark chocolate bowls (but not the white).

Microwave each one for 20 seconds and stir, then microwave again for 10 seconds and stir. Continue until completely melted, but keep your eye on the chocolate as it can easily burn.

Put the sprinkles and nuts into small bowls, then arrange with the chocolate bowls and ice lollies on the bonanza table and let the kids start dipping!

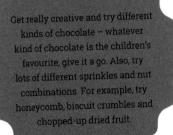

TIP!

Get really creative and try different kinds of chocolate – whatever kind of chocolate is the children's favourite, give it a go. Also, try lots of different sprinkles and nut combinations. For example, try honeycomb, biscuit crumbles and chopped-up dried fruit.

BANANA SPLIT

A frozen lolly twist on this classic dessert.

SERVES	PREP	FREEZING
4	**10** MINS	**6** HRS

OR OVERNIGHT

170g banana, peeled and chopped

130ml whole milk

4 teaspoons natural unrefined sugar

a small handful of milk chocolate chips

a small bowl of chopped mixed nuts

50g milk chocolate, broken into pieces

1 teaspoon coconut oil

Whizz together the banana, milk and sugar in a blender. Divide the mixture between the moulds, leaving a 2cm gap at the top. Sprinkle in the chocolate chips and half the chopped nuts. Using a spare lolly stick, arrange the nuts and chocolate chips evenly.

Top up each mould with the banana mixture, leaving a 1cm gap at the top. Insert the sticks with the stick-holders and place in the freezer.

When the lollies are fully frozen, put the chocolate pieces into a microwavable container with the coconut oil. Microwave for 20 seconds and stir, then microwave again for 10 seconds and stir. Continue until completely melted, but keep your eye on the chocolate as it can easily burn.

De-mould one lolly at a time and dip into the melted chocolate; allow the excess chocolate to drip off, then dip the lolly into the bowl of chopped nuts. Wait until the chocolate has set then serve, or return to the freezer until ready. Repeat with the other lollies.

TIP

Lactose intolerant or vegan? Try swapping the whole milk with almond or coconut milk.

OVER THE RAINBOW

A fruity mixed-layer rainbow lolly! This takes quite a lot of time to make, but it's worth it for the end result. Waiting for the different layers to freeze takes time, so try to make these while you are home one day.

SERVES 4   **PREP** 15 MINS   **FREEZING** 3 HRS

FOR EACH LAYER

30g strawberries, hulled and chopped

60ml orange juice

30g pineapple, peeled and chopped

30g kiwi, peeled and chopped

30g blackberries, chopped

1¼ teaspoons natural unrefined sugar

To make each layer, whizz together each fruit in a blender with 30ml of water and ¼ teaspoon of sugar – except for the orange: add just the sugar and whizz until dissolved.

Pour each layer one-fifth of the way up each mould, adding the layers in the same order as the fruits are listed in the ingredients. Freeze each layer for about 3 hours.

Place the sticks in the first or second layer, depending on how far out you want the stick to protrude from the base of the lolly. Put the stick-holders on top and place in the freezer. After the sticks have frozen into place there is no need to replace the stick-holders each time. When adding a new layer, pour carefully so you don't pour the mixture on the part of the stick you will hold.

When you pour the final blackberry layer into the mould, leave a 1cm gap at the top. Place in the freezer until ready to serve.

TIP

When de-moulding a layered lolly, make sure you get warm water all the way up the sides and around the moulds, so none of the layers get stuck.

PB&J

It's a peanut butter and strawberry jam sandwich on a stick!

SERVES | PREP | FREEZING
4 | 10 MINS | 6 HRS
| | OR OVERNIGHT

160g strawberries, hulled and chopped

2 teaspoons natural unrefined cane sugar

40g smooth peanut butter

2–3 teaspoons strawberry jam

Put the strawberries, sugar and 20ml of water in a blender, whizz together and set aside in a jug.

Put the peanut butter and 40ml of water in the blender, whizz together and set aside in another jug.

Pour a little bit of the strawberry mixture, then the peanut butter mixture into the moulds and after every few pours add a small dollop of jam, about ¼ teaspoon. Don't add in more than a teaspoon of jam per mould or the lolly won't freeze properly.

Top up the moulds with the rest of the mixture, leaving a 1cm gap at the top.

Insert the sticks with the stick-holders and place in the freezer.

FUN FACT

The jam doesn't actually freeze!

WATERMELON PIZZA

Wow the kids with this fantastic and colourful dessert. Or, better still, turn it into a party game and have all the kids decorate their own fruit 'pizza'.

SERVES 4-8   **PREP** 20 MINS   **FREEZING** 0 HRS

PER PIZZA, DEPENDING ON SIZE OF WATERMELON

1 whole watermelon

kiwis, peeled and cut into small pieces

blueberries, either whole or chopped

strawberries, hulled and cut into small pieces

1 peach, pitted and cut into small pieces

desiccated coconut

mint (optional)

Cut the watermelon in half and then cut a few 2–3cm wide whole slices from the centre of the watermelon – so that they resemble pizza bases. Pick out the seeds, if desired.

Cut the slices before you add the toppings, as this makes it easier to serve up.

Create the pizza on the plate that you will serve it on. Simply start to top the watermelon slice with pieces of fruit, as you would if you were topping a traditional pizza.

Try lots of different fruit combinations – the more the better. Sprinkle with desiccated coconut to resemble cheese, and mint, if you like.

TIP!

Want to add 'tomato sauce'? Try spreading the watermelon slices with your favourite yogurt, then add the fruity toppings.

FROZEN FRUITY KEBABS

A fun way to get some delicious and healthy fruit into a kids' party or just as a snack for the whole family. Try getting the kids involved and get them to make their own fruit kebab and wrap a piece of tape with their name written on it so you know whose is whose.

SERVES **4**   PREP **10** MINS   FREEZING **4** HRS
OR OVERNIGHT

a variety of fruit chunks (we used strawberries, star fruit, bananas, red grapes, kiwis, mango and pineapple)

First, check whether your skewers will fit in your freezer. If they don't, cut them to size.

Load up the fruit on the skewers. It is best to start with a firm fruit to prevent all the fruit sliding off.

Consider the order in which you want to add the fruit; it's all about making the kebabs look super-appetizing to eat.

Place in the freezer on greaseproof paper or on a tray.

TIP!

Feeling naughty? Try drizzling the kebabs with melted chocolate. Or, instead of freezing, pop them on the BBQ for a few minutes for a warm, caramelised dessert!

HEALTHY
KICKS

BEETROOT, CARROT & ORANGE

This lolly helps keep our bones, teeth, skin and eyes healthy. Carrots are full of beta-carotene, which our bodies turn into vitamin A. Also, research has shown that beetroot juice may help lower blood pressure.

SERVES 4

PREP 5 MINS

FREEZING 6 HRS

OR OVERNIGHT

40ml beetroot juice

100ml carrot juice

140ml orange juice

20g red grapes, (optional, if you want to sweeten the lollies)

Put all the ingredients in a blender and whizz together.

Divide the mixture between the moulds, leaving a 1cm gap at the top.

Insert the sticks with the stick-holders and place in the freezer.

FUN FACT

The colour of beetroot comes from betacyanin, which is an antioxidant and helps to stimulate the liver's detoxification process. Could be a good lolly for the morning after!

HEALTHY KICKS

74

ORANGE, CARROT & GINGER

This lolly is full of vitamins A, B, C and K. Also, ginger is known for aiding digestion, reducing inflammation, and helping to relieve pain and nausea.

SERVES 4

PREP 5 MINS

FREEZING 6 HRS OR OVERNIGHT

120ml carrot juice

120ml orange juice

1 teaspoon peeled and grated fresh ginger

4 small pinches (about 1/8 teaspoon) of ground ginger

Put all the ingredients in a blender and whizz together.

If you love ginger and want the lollies to pack a punch, add more of both types of ginger to your desired taste.

Divide the mixture between the moulds, leaving a 1cm gap at the top.

Insert the sticks with the stick-holders and place in the freezer.

TIP!

Do you like things sweet? Reduce the orange and carrot juice by 30ml each and add 60g of green grapes instead to sweeten the lollies without adding any sugar.

FENNEL ICED TEA

Fennel seeds have long been used in traditional medicines to aid digestion. They contain powerful antioxidants, essential oil compounds, minerals and vitamins. Fennel seeds are actually the fruit of the plant!

SERVES 4 PREP 7 MINS FREEZING 6 HRS
OR OVERNIGHT

1 teaspoon fennel seeds

160ml boiling water

160ml freshly squeezed orange juice

2 teaspoons honey

Steep the fennel seeds in the boiling water in a mug for 5 minutes.

Strain the fennel tea into the blender through a fine sieve. Add the remaining ingredients and whizz together.

Divide the mixture between the moulds, leaving a 1cm gap at the top. Insert the sticks with the stick-holders and place in the freezer.

GRAPEALICIOUS

This lolly is incredibly quick to make – just another refreshing way to get more fruit into your diet. Grapes are naturally high in sugar, so they are the perfect fruit to give you your sweet fix but in a natural and healthy way. (So head for the freezer instead of the snack cupboard next time!)

SERVES 4 PREP 5 MINS FREEZING 6 HRS
OR OVERNIGHT

200g red grapes (or try using black or green grapes to mix up the colours)

Put the grapes and 100ml of water in a blender and whizz together.

Divide the mixture between the moulds, leaving a 1cm gap at the top. Insert the sticks with the stick-holders and place in the freezer.

ROASTED PINEAPPLE & HONEY

This recipe requires an oven. By baking the pineapple with honey you get a caramelised taste without adding extra sugar.

SERVES | PREP | FREEZING

4 | **35** MINS | **6** HRS

OR OVERNIGHT

160g peeled and chopped pineapple

1 teaspoon clear honey

Preheat the oven to 180°C/gas mark 4.

Place the pineapple on a baking tray and drizzle with the honey. Bake for about 30 minutes, or until the pineapple is caramelised. Remove from the oven and leave to cool.

Put the cooled, roasted pineapple and 160ml of water in a blender and whizz together.

Divide the mixture between the moulds, leaving a 1cm gap at the top.

Insert the sticks with the stick-holders and place in the freezer.

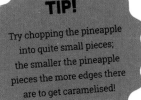

TIP!

Try chopping the pineapple into quite small pieces; the smaller the pineapple pieces the more edges there are to get caramelised!

ALMOND, CHIA & RASPBERRY

You will get lots of nutrients from this lolly. The almond milk contains vitamin E, which is great for your skin. Chia seeds contain calcium, magnesium, phosphorus and protein, which are essential for good bones. Chia seeds are also full of antioxidants, fibre, zinc and iron.

SERVES 4 **PREP** 5 MINS **FREEZING** 6 HRS

OR OVERNIGHT

260ml almond milk

2 teaspoons chia seeds

a handful of raspberries

In a jug, mix together the almond milk and chia seeds.

Divide the mixture between the moulds, leaving a 3cm gap at the top.

Cut the raspberries in half and place some in each mould. Using a spare lolly stick, arrange the raspberries, if needed.

Top up each mould with the almond milk mixture, leaving a 1cm gap at the top.

Insert the sticks with the stick-holders and place in the freezer.

FUN FACTS

Almond milk contains healthy fats and it doesn't have any cholesterol or saturated fat.

By weight, chia seeds are 40 per cent fibre, which means they are one of the best sources of fibre!

BERRY YOGURT SWIRLS

Ever wanted to have a lolly for breakfast? This healthy breakfast alternative is the perfect excuse to do just that.

SERVES 4

PREP 10 MINS

FREEZING 6 HRS
OR OVERNIGHT

140g natural yogurt

40g sugar-free granola, plus extra for sprinkling

40g blueberries

20g raspberries

20g strawberries, hulled and chopped

In a bowl, mix together the yogurt and granola. Then put the blueberries and 40ml of water in a blender, whizz together and transfer to a bowl. Finally, put the raspberries, strawberries and 40ml of water in the blender, whizz together and set aside in a separate bowl.

Divide the mixtures between each mould, starting with the yogurt mix, by pouring or spooning them and layering as you go. Leave a 1cm gap at the top of each one, finishing each lolly with a layer of yogurt.

Sprinkle a little extra granola on the top of each mould and lightly press down so the granola sticks to the yogurt when de-moulded.

Insert the sticks with the stick-holders and place in the freezer.

TIP!
Choose your favourite sugar-free yogurt or add a drizzle of clear honey between the layers.

BANANA & PEANUT STACKS

These make the perfect little snack when you are feeling a bit peckish. These stacks have slow-releasing energy, perfect to get you through to the next meal.

SERVES

MANY AS
LITTLE SNACKS

PREP

10
MINS

FREEZING

3
HRS

2 bananas, peeled and sliced about 1cm thick

a jar of smooth or crunchy peanut butter

a few pieces of dark chocolate

½ teaspoon coconut oil

TRY THIS
For extra crunch, add some chia seeds on top of the peanut butter, or a couple of cacao nibs.

Place a sheet of greaseproof paper on a metal tray that fits into your freezer. Sandwich some peanut butter between two discs of banana to make a stack and place on the tray; repeat until you have used all the banana.

Put the chocolate and coconut oil in a small microwavable bowl or mug. Microwave for 30 seconds, stir and keep on melting for 10 seconds at a time until the chocolate has melted. Keep checking the chocolate, as it can easily burn.

Use a teaspoon to drizzle the chocolate over each banana stack.

Place the tray in the freezer and, once frozen, transfer the mini stacks into an airtight container and keep in the freezer for when you need a snack.

COCONUT WATER SURPRISE

Coconut water is a great source of hydration for your body. It is naturally isotonic and contains electrolytes, minerals and simple sugars. It also has many naturally occurring bioactive enzymes, which help digestion and metabolism.

SERVES **4**

PREP **5** MINS

FREEZING **6** HRS

OR OVERNIGHT

280ml unsweetened coconut water

a small handful of different diced fruit (see Tip)

Divide the coconut water between the moulds and sprinkle in some of the small fruit pieces, leaving a 1cm gap at the top.

Use a spare lolly stick to rearrange the fruit pieces so that they are evenly distributed, if required.

Insert the sticks with the stick-holders and place in the freezer.

TIP!
Choose different fruits to add to the coconut water, such as strawberry, kiwi and mango. Each of these add different flavour bites throughout the lolly and a great mix of colour.

GREEN GODDESS

Get an extra bit of spinach in your diet by having one of these lollies. Not only do they look amazing, but spinach is also a superfood, packed with nutrients and low in calories. It's one of the best sources of potassium and magnesium, which help your metabolism and immune system.

SERVES	PREP	FREEZING
4	5 MINS	6 HRS
		OR OVERNIGHT

140g pineapple, peeled and chopped

140ml apple juice

40g spinach

12 mint leaves

2 teaspoons freshly squeezed lemon juice

Put all the ingredients in a blender and whizz together until you reach the consistency you want.

Divide the mixture between the moulds, leaving a 1cm gap at the top.

Insert the sticks with the stick-holders and place in the freezer.

TIP!
Need some extra sweetness?
Add 2 teaspoons of honey.

FUN FACT
Did you know that most of the calories in spinach come from protein?

FRUITY YOGURT BITES

Try making these with mini cupcake cases for breakfast. Just add to muesli or granola as an extra yummy topping!

SERVES

PREP
10 MINS

FREEZING
4 HRS

SERVES
AS MANY AS
YOU LIKE

OR OVERNIGHT

natural yogurt

fruit cut into small pieces

a variety of seeds (we used pumpkin, flax, chia, sunflower and poppy)

cupcake cases (we find the smaller, shallow ones work best)

Place the cupcake cases on a tray (ensure it fits in your freezer).

Spoon some yogurt into each case, leaving room to add some fruit and seeds. Spoon your preferred mixture of fruit and seeds on top of the yogurt.

Place the tray in the freezer on a flat surface and, once frozen, transfer the bites into an airtight container and keep in the freezer for when you need a snack.

Topping combinations that we find work well together are:
• Strawberries and peaches
• Berries and seeds
• Mango and kiwi
• Banana and chia
• Apricot and peach
• Strawberry, banana and poppy seeds

Basically, have a go with anything you can think of!

COCKTAIL
CORNER

RASPBERRY MOJITO

The history of the mojito can be traced as far back as the 1500s, making it one of the oldest mixed drinks still consumed today. So, mix things up and serve your friends mojitos on a stick!

SERVES
4

PREP
5 MINS

FREEZING
6 HRS

OR OVERNIGHT

200g raspberries

4 teaspoons white rum

4 teaspoons natural unrefined sugar

8 mint leaves

2 teaspoons freshly squeezed lime juice

Put all the ingredients and 80ml of water in a blender and whizz together.

Divide the mixture between the moulds, leaving a 1cm gap at the top.

Insert the sticks with the stick-holders and place in the freezer.

FUN FACTS

Did you know that in the 1800s, rum was used to clean hair and help strengthen its roots?

The colour of rum is determined by its ageing process.

PEACH BELLINI

A new and fun way to serve delicious lollies and your favourite bubbly to your friends... It's also a great way to keep your cocktail cold!

SERVES **PREP** **FREEZING**

4 | 5 MINS | 6 HRS

OR OVERNIGHT

200g white peaches, stoned and chopped (it's best to keep the skin on, but remove if you prefer)

4 teaspoons natural unrefined sugar

1 bottle of prosecco, chilled

4 large wine glasses

Put the peaches, sugar and 100ml of water in a blender and whizz together.

Divide the mixture between the moulds, leaving a 1cm gap at the top.

Insert the sticks with the stick-holders and place in the freezer.

When frozen, de-mould and store until ready to use.

To serve, place each lolly in a wine glass and pour over the prosecco.

As your guests stir their lollies, they can watch the prosecco turn into the famous cocktail, but with a lolly twist!

TIP!

Make sure the lolly will fit into the wine glass you are using.

FUN FACT

Bellinis originated in Venice, Italy!

ZESTY MARGARITA

For a sharp and refreshing poptail, try this recipe; it is perfect to get everyone in the party mood or to cool them down on a hot day.

SERVES **4**   PREP **5** MINS   FREEZING **6** HRS

OR OVERNIGHT

7 teaspoons freshly squeezed lime juice

4 teaspoons tequila

8 teaspoons natural unrefined sugar

a tiny pinch of salt

Put all the ingredients and 200ml of water in a blender and whizz together.

Divide the mixture between the moulds, leaving a 1cm gap at the top.

Insert the sticks with the stick-holders and place in the freezer.

FUN FACTS

Margarita means daisy in Spanish.

Tequila is made from the blue agave plant.

WHITE RUSSIAN

Another classic cocktail twisted onto a stick. Try this one for your coffee- and cocktail-loving friends.

SERVES	PREP	FREEZING
4	10 MINS	6 HRS
		OR OVERNIGHT

2 pinches of instant coffee

160ml hot water

2 teaspoons Kahlúa

6 teaspoons natural unrefined sugar

160ml whole milk

2 teaspoons vodka

Put the coffee, hot water, Kahlúa and 3 teaspoons of the sugar in a blender and whizz together, then set aside to cool.

Put the milk, vodka and remaining sugar in a separate bowl and mix.

You can pour the two mixtures into the moulds at the same time, or pour the coffee first then gently pour the milk down the sides of the moulds. The two parts will mix but not entirely. Divide the mixtures between the moulds, leaving a 1cm gap at the top.

Insert the sticks with the stick-holders and place in the freezer.

TIP!

Want to indulge? Swap half the milk for cream.

CHOCOLATE BANANA DAIQUIRI

This daiquiri has a cheeky chocolate kick!

SERVES 4

PREP 10 MINS.

FREEZING 6 HRS

OR OVERNIGHT

180g banana, peeled

4 teaspoons white rum

4 teaspoons natural unrefined sugar

50g dark chocolate, broken into pieces

½ teaspoon coconut oil

Put the banana, rum, sugar and 100ml of water in a blender and whizz together.

Divide the mixture between the moulds, leaving a 1cm gap at the top. Insert the sticks with the stick-holders and place in the freezer.

When frozen, de-mould the lollies and store until ready to use.

When you want to serve the lollies, put the chocolate into a microwavable bowl, add the coconut oil and microwave for 20 seconds, then stir. Microwave again for 10 seconds and stir. Continue until completely melted, but keep your eye on the chocolate as it can easily burn.

Either dip each lolly into the bowl or drizzle the chocolate over each lolly. Hold the lolly while the chocolate sets, and either serve straight away or store in the freezer.

FUN FACT

Daiquiri is the name of a beach in Cuba.

SPICED RUM PLUM

This is great to make when plums are in season. We use red plums as they give a fantastic flavour, but use whatever plums you have. Spiced rums are usually flavoured with cinnamon, rosemary, anise, absinthe, pepper or caramel.

SERVES
4

PREP
5 MINS

FREEZING
6 HRS

OR OVERNIGHT

200g red plums, stoned and chopped

4 teaspoons spiced rum

4–8 teaspoons natural unrefined sugar

4 pinches (about ¼ teaspoon) each of ground cinnamon and nutmeg

Put all the ingredients and 80ml of water in a blender and whizz together. The amount of sugar to use will depend on how sweet or tart your plums are.

Divide the mixture between the moulds, leaving a 1cm gap at the top.

Insert the sticks with the stick-holders and place in the freezer.

STRAWBERRY SAMBUCA

Do you love aniseed and liquorice? Then this poptail is for you, with an added spicy kick. Sambuca originates from Italy.

SERVES
4

PREP
5 MINS

FREEZING
6 HRS

OR OVERNIGHT

200g strawberries, hulled and chopped

4 teaspoons sambuca

4 teaspoons natural unrefined sugar

a good pinch of ground black pepper

Put all the ingredients and 80ml of water in a blender and whizz together.

Divide the mixture between the moulds, leaving a 1cm gap at the top. Insert the sticks with the stick-holders and place in the freezer.

CHERRY MARTINI

Shaken or stirred? No, I'll take mine with fresh cherries instead!
You shouldn't actually shake a martini because it bruises the gin!

SERVES **PREP** **FREEZING**

4   10 MINS   6 HRS

OR OVERNIGHT

200g cherries, stoned and chopped

2 teaspoons gin, or vodka if you don't like gin

2 teaspoons dry vermouth

4 teaspoons natural unrefined sugar

Put all the ingredients and 100ml of water in a blender and whizz together.

Divide the mixture between the moulds, leaving a 1cm gap at the top.

Insert the sticks with the stick-holders and place in the freezer.

GIN SLING

A refreshing poptail for those who like things a little on the sour side.

SERVES **PREP** **FREEZING**

4   5 MINS   6 HRS

OR OVERNIGHT

240g pink or red grapefruit, peeled, pith removed and chopped

4 teaspoons gin

8 teaspoons natural unrefined sugar

Put all the ingredients in a blender and whizz together.

Divide the mixture between the moulds, leaving a 1cm gap at the top.

Insert the sticks with the stick-holders and place in the freezer.

BLOODY MARY

This poptail is for those who love a savoury snack with a bit of heat.
It may sound a little bit crazy to make a lolly out of tomatoes,
but it works... give it a try.

SERVES 4 **PREP** 5 MINS **FREEZING** 6 HRS

FOR EACH LAYER

300g tomatoes

40g celery

4 teaspoons vodka

3 teaspoons natural unrefined sugar

4 dashes of Tabasco

4 small pinches (about ⅛ teaspoon) of salt

Put all the ingredients in a blender and whizz together.

Divide the mixture between the moulds, leaving a 1cm gap at the top.

Insert the sticks with the stick-holders and place in the freezer.

TIP!

Add more Tabasco if you want the lollies to have an extra kick!

FUN FACT

Our bodies are able to absorb more helpful nutrients from cooked tomatoes.

INDEX

THANK YOU!

There are really too many people to fit on one page to thank for the success of LICKALIX and this book but there are a few people we had to mention.

Thank you to our loving and supportive parents and our sister Rachel. Without them we would not have been able to make the leap of faith to start LICKALIX and follow our dreams.

Thank you to our amazing friends who are like our family; we couldn't have accomplished what we have without you.

Thank you to Caroline and the team at London Fields Lido in London. They were the first ones to give us a go and sell our lollies. Because of them we have die-hard fans that will always order a LICKALIX lolly.

A big thanks to Team LICKALIX (Hana, Safaa and Sotiri amongst many); for all their hard work, inspiration, good humour and continued devotion to the lolly cause.

Thanks to our awesome book team who made this book what it is.

Lastly, thank you for everyone who has bought this book, tried to make a more natural and healthier treat and joined the lolly revolution with us!

Lots of lolly love

Karis & Dominic

First published in
Great Britain in 2016 by
Kyle Books, an imprint of Kyle Cathie Ltd
192–198 Vauxhall Bridge Road
London SW1V 1DX
general.enquiries@kylebooks.com
www.kylebooks.co.uk

10 9 8 7 6 5 4 3 2 1

ISBN 978 0 85783 356 3

Project Editor: Claire Rogers
Copy Editor: Suzanne Dickerson
Designer: Nicky Collings
Photographer: Rita Platts
Stylist: Sam Dixon
Prop Stylist: Louie Waller
Production: Nic Jones and
Gemma John

A Cataloguing in Publication record for this
title is available from the British Library.

Colour reproduction by ALTA London
Printed and bound in China by 1010 International
Printing Ltd.

All servings are based on 80ml lolly moulds